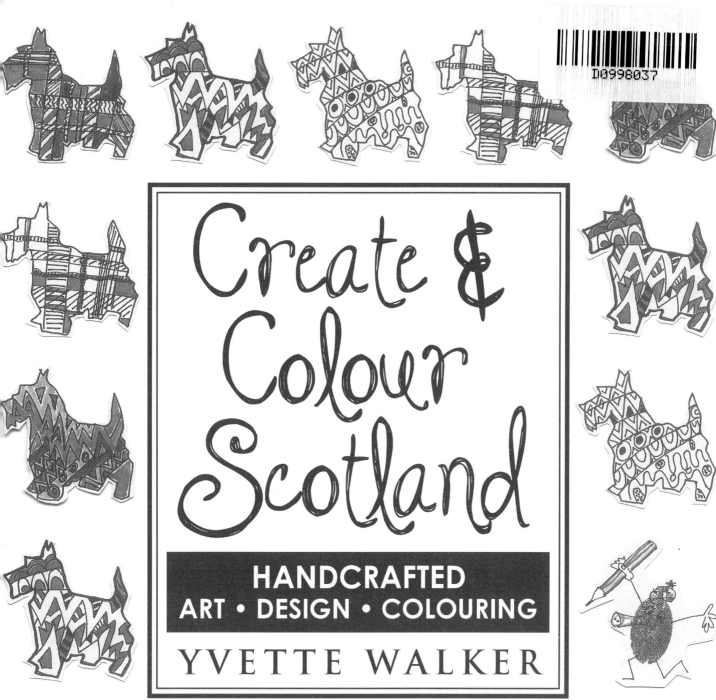

Create & Colour Scotland

HANDCRAFTED
ART • DESIGN • COLOURING

YVETTE WALKER

BLACK & WHITE PUBLISHING

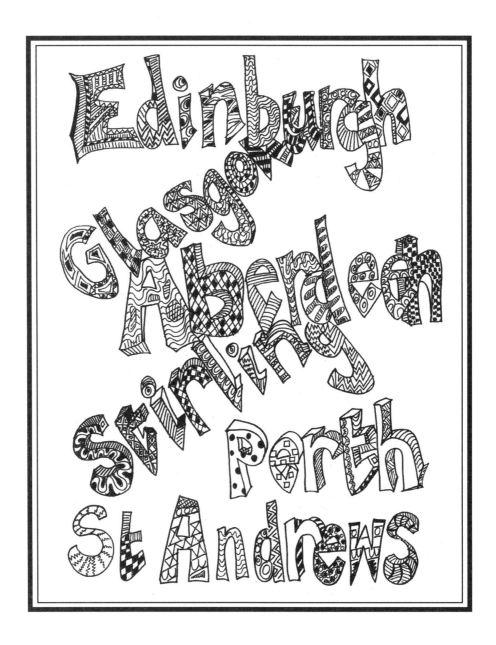

First published 2015
by Black & White Publishing Ltd
29 Ocean Drive, Edinburgh EH6 6JL

1 3 5 7 9 10 8 6 4 2   15 16 17 18

ISBN: 978 1 78530 017 2

Typeset by Creative Link, North Berwick
Printed and bound in Poland by www.hussarbooks.pl

This book is packed full of art and design activities with a very Scottish flair. It shows you how to design your own tartan, reinvent a Paisley pattern or experiment with paper weaving.

Through drawing you can find out about Charles Rennie Mackintosh, create your own version of The Monarch of the Glen, draw a simple version of a Westie and lots more. All the activities have been broken down into easy steps to make the learning fun.

This book is for all ages as anyone can draw. Enjoy!!

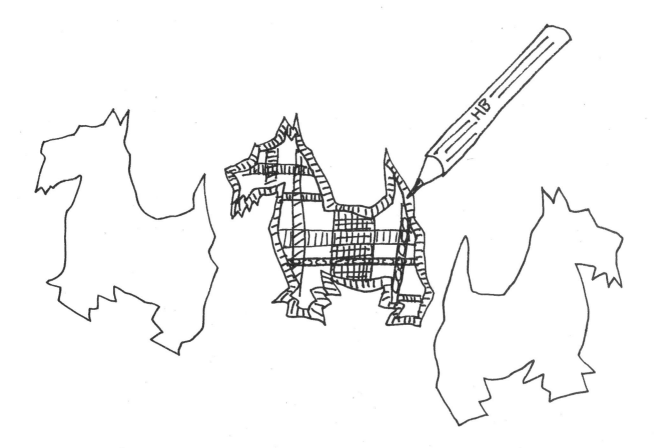

Drawing with pencil

Today pencils are usually lettered
and numbered to tell us how
hard the lead is.
Soft leads are labelled with a 'B'
for black.
Harder leads are labelled with an
'H' for hard.

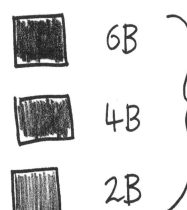

6B
4B
2B

} These are soft pencils
often used by artists
for drawing, sketching
and hatching.

HB — Standard writing pencil

2H
4H

} These are harder pencils
often used for more
technical subjects.

Practise making these pencil marks

hatching	
cross hatching	
stippling	
combe	
tonal grading	
pebble texture	
grass texture	
grass/pebble combination	

Scotland has many amazing castles. Experiment with pencil to create your own fantastic castle. →

Building a castle

Start with a square or rectangular shape with a saw tooth pattern at the top.

Design a grand entrance.

Use rectangles and square shapes to add extensions onto the castle.

Experiment by giving some of the buildings triangular roofs. Add different window designs. Add more detail.

Design your own castle

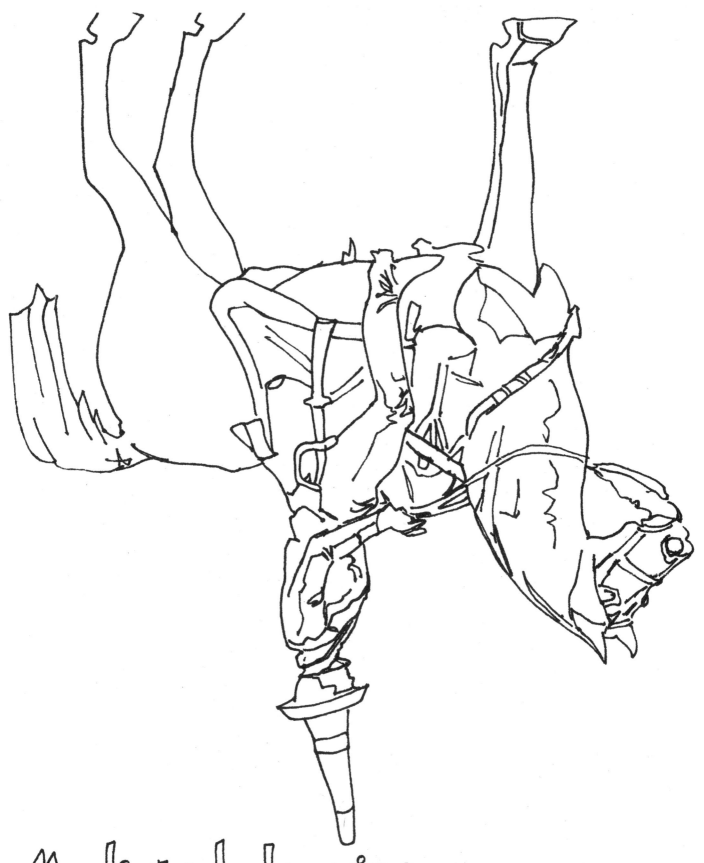

Mediated drawing

Mediated or upside-down drawings of famous works of art can help you to look at something in a different way. Without turning the book the other way round try copying this image of a famous Scottish sculpture.

When you have completed your drawing turn it the right way up!

Observation Drawing

This is an observational drawing of a can of Baxters soup, a well-known Scottish brand. An observational drawing requires the artist to really examine what is in front of them and try to draw and make sense of what they see.

Draw something in front of you. Really examine the object and draw what you see. Remember a drawing is just a series of lines. Everyone can draw. The more you practise drawing the better you get.

Finish this picture anyway you like.

Edinburgh Castle

Colour this image.

A corrie-fisted (left handed) piper.

Inspired by The Heart of Midlothian create your own heart design.

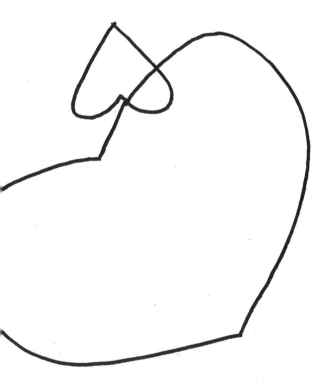

The Heart of Midlothian on the Royal Mile in Edinburgh marks the site of a tolbooth or prison, where executions took place. Folk would spit on the Heart to show their disdain though nowadays this is said to bring good luck.

Drawing the eye

Step 1.

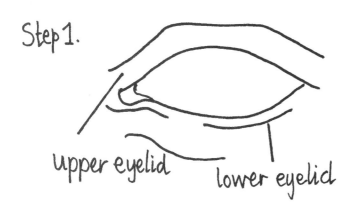

upper eyelid   lower eyelid

Lightly sketch the almond shape of the eye with a double line at the bottom.

Step 2.

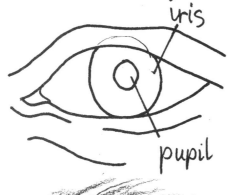

iris

pupil

Draw the iris sitting on the lower eyelid. Note the iris is partially covered by the upper eyelid.

Step 3.

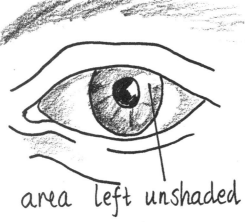

area left unshaded

To make the eye look glassy leave a small area unshaded. The pupil should be the darkest. The iris is darker round the edge.

Step 4.

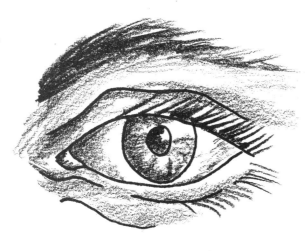

Finish shading around the eye. Finally add eyebrows and eyelashes paying attention to the direction of their growth.

Use pencil to practise drawing
your own eyes

"Och aye the noo"

Drawing a face

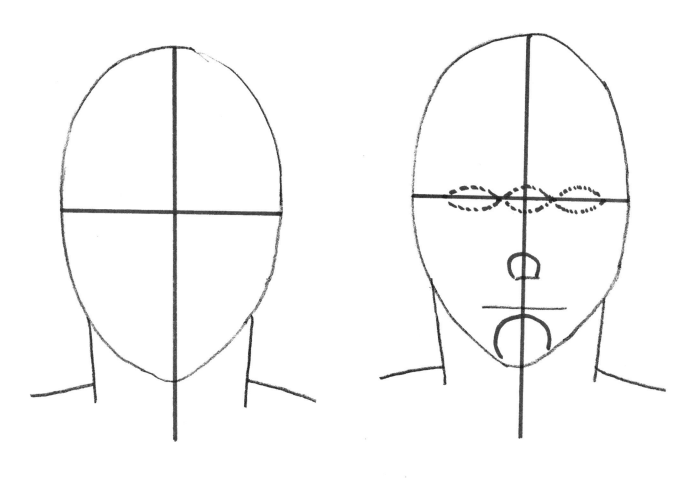

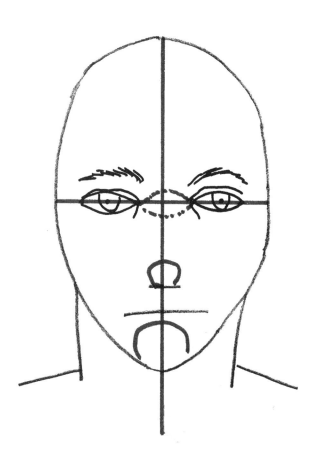

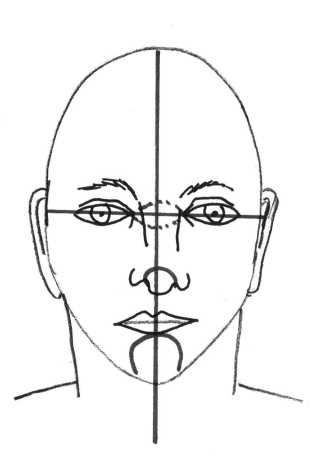

Now complete this face

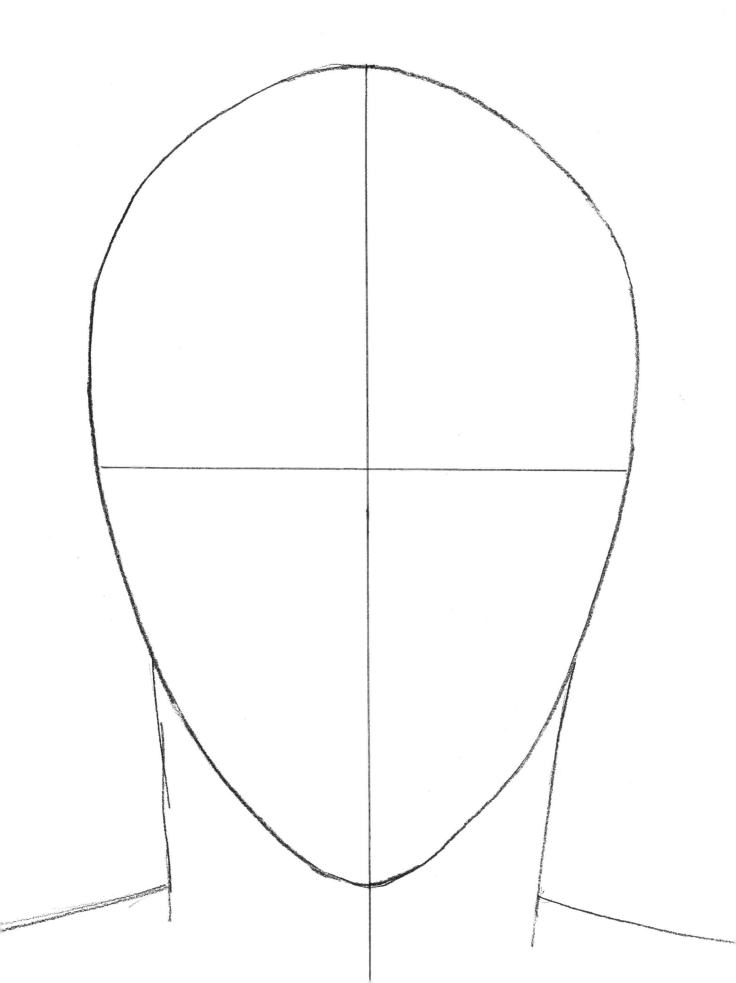

Now that you can draw a face, experiment with light and shade

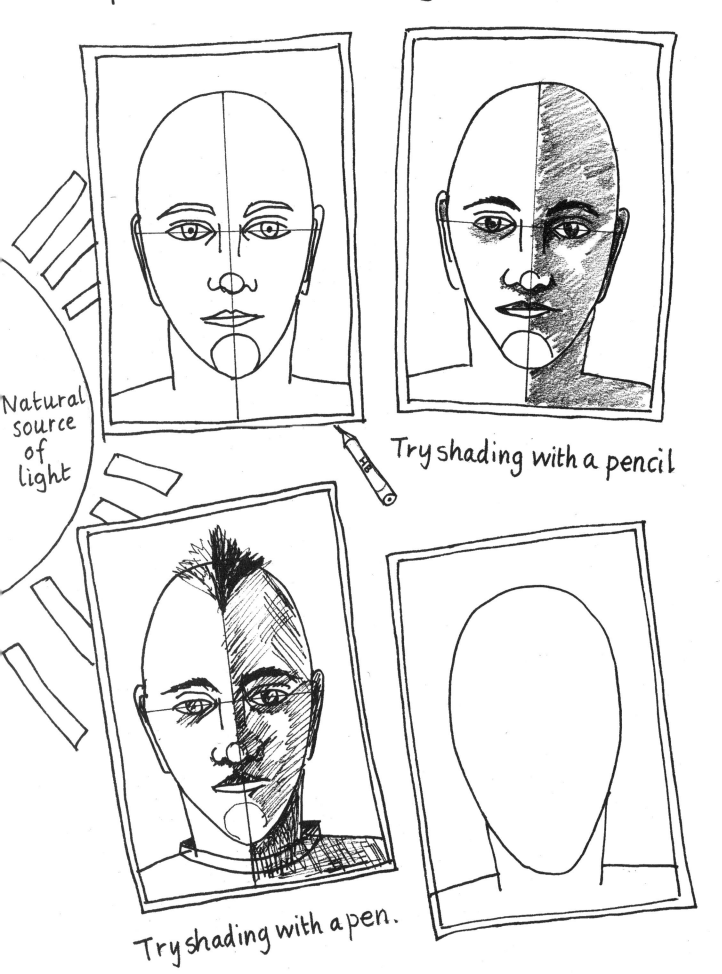

Natural source of light

Try shading with a pencil

Try shading with a pen.

Draw some more Scottish folk

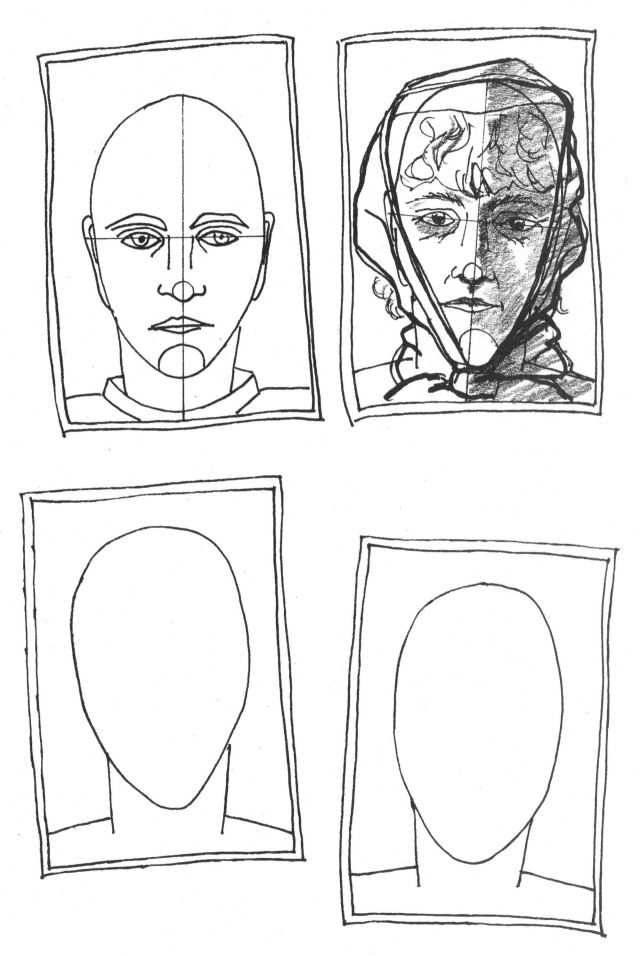

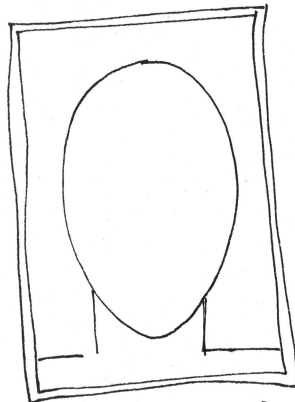

Draw more Scottish folk

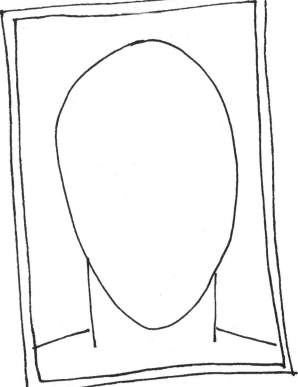

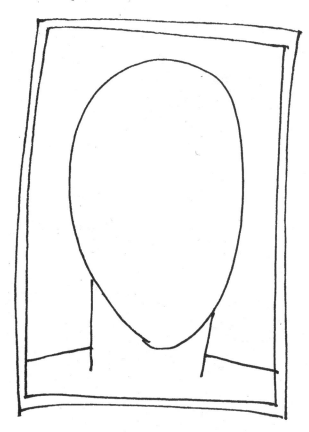

Try adding shade.

Try adding colour.

Decorate each Westie to create your own unique design.

SCOTTISH TERRIERS AND WEST HIGHLAND WHITE TERRIERS

DESIGN SOME SCOTTISH POSTCARDS OF YOUR OWN.

Wish you were here

Souvenirs from Scotland

Tartan Patterns

Tartan is a pattern made up of criss-crossed vertical and horizontal bands of colour. Scotland has become famous for its tartan designs. The tartan kilt is part of Scotland's national costume. The kilt can be worn by both men and women. Originally tartans were linked to the area or district of Scotland in which they were made. However, by the mid-nineteenth century tartans were designed to represent a specific institution, family, or clan, as they are known in Scotland.

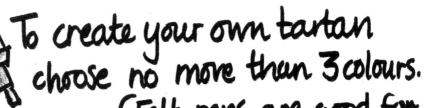

To create your own tartan choose no more than 3 colours. (Felt pens are good for this task.)

Draw horizontal lines of different thicknesses, using all 3 colours.

Use the same 3 pens to draw vertical stripes of different thicknesses.

Design some more tartan patterns.

The Floating

Heads

in Glasgow's

Kelvingrove was designed by Sir John W Simpson in the Spanish Baroque style and is built using the traditional Glaswegian red sandstone from Locharbriggs.

Kelvingrove Museum

Designed by a company called Event Creation, this installation was chosen to represent the concept of 'expression'.

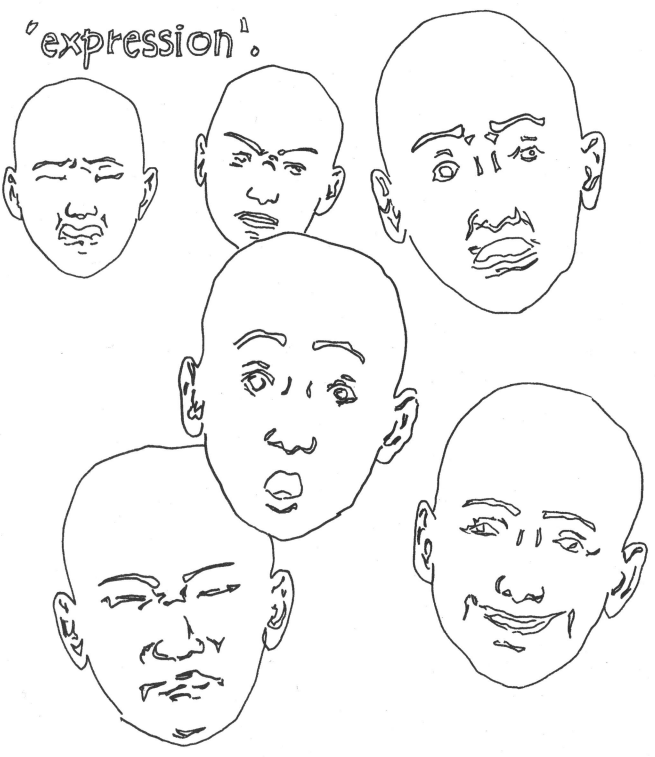

Draw expressions on the faces
The Floating Heads.

to create your own version of

CHARLES RENNIE MACKINTOSH

was born in Glasgow 1868-1928 and died in London.

Charles Rennie Mackintosh was an architect, artist, designer and water colourist. He was the leader of the Art Nouveau style in Britain. Examples of his work can still be seen in and around the city of Glasgow.

GLASGOW DESIGN

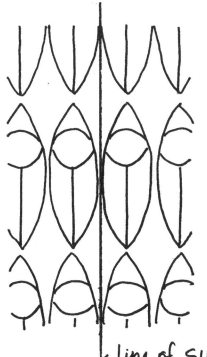

The work of Charles Rennie Mackintosh often contained strong right angles, floral motifs and subtle curves. He made strong use of symmetry in his work. Many of his designs were the same on both sides.

←line of symmetry

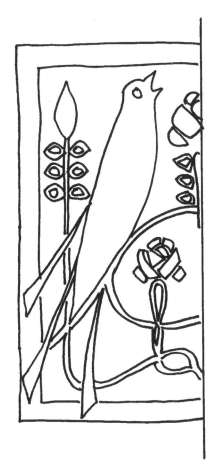

Draw the mirror image of this Mackintosh design.

CHARLES RENNIE MACKINTOSH used symmetry

when he designed The Scotland Street Museum.
Complete the design.

– line of symmetry

GLASGOW SCHOOL OF ART

is recognised as Mackintosh's greatest achievement. It is not symmetrical. His work was ahead of its time. It was very modern yet very functional.

MACKINTOSH CHAIRS

line of symmetry

Mackintosh made use of symmetry when designing his furniture. Complete this design.

Think of unusual ways to colour The Glasgow Rose

CHARLES RENNIE MACKINTOSH

HANDWRITING PATTERNS FOR YOU TO COMPLETE...

ABCDEFGHIJKLMNOP
QRSTUVWXYZ

Try experimenting with letters to create some different repeating patterns.

_____

_____

_____

_____

_____

_____

_____

_____

_____

_____

_____

_____

How to draw a 'dug' story

Many children are taught to draw a simple dog using this story. You may know a different version.

There was once a wee man with no arms or face.

He was attacked by midges...

... so he ran to a pool and jumped in.

In the background there was a hill...

...with two smaller hills infront.

In each hill there was a dark cave.

Along each side there was a loch.

Use the story to draw your own version of a 'dug.'

THE CLYDE CLOCK
by George Wylie

Often referred to as
the 'Running Man', the
Clyde Clock was gifted
to Glasgow by Radio Clyde
to celebrate their 25th
anniversary of broadcasting.
It was designed as a
meeting point and chimes
once a day at 8pm, an
ideal meeting time.

Try
designing
your own
clock
sculpture

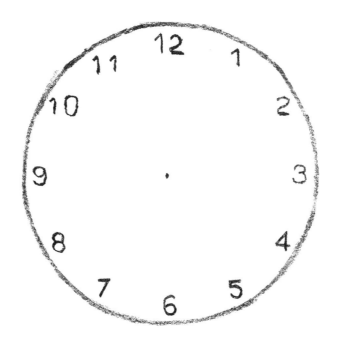

PAISLEY PATTERN OR BOTEH DESIGNS

THE PAISLEY PATTERN OR BOTEH
DESIGN RESEMBLES A TWISTED TEAR-
DROP. THE DESIGN ORIGINALLY CAME
FROM INDIA AND IRAN BUT BECAME
POPULAR IN THE WEST DURING THE 18th
AND 19th CENTURY. THE PATTERN TAKES
ITS MODERN NAME FROM THE SCOTTISH
TOWN OF PAISLEY WHICH BECAME FAMOUS FOR PRINTING
PAISLEY PATTERN TEXTILES IN THE EARLY 19th CENTURY.

Decorate your own boteh design

add colour

Finish this Paisley design

colour this paisley design

Sir Walter Scott (1771-1832)
novelist/playwright
and poet

Finish

James VI of Scotland and
James I of England

Famous
Scots

James Watt (1736 - 1819) known for his invention of the steam engine.

Greyfriars Bobby - a Skye Terrier, who spent 14 years guarding the grave of his owner until he died on 14th January 1872.

Alexander Graham Bell (1847-1922)

inventor of the
telephone

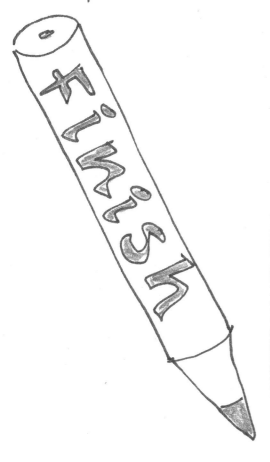

Hamish McHamish - a ginger
cat that lived in the town of
St Andrews in Fife. He became
famous after a book was
written about him, entitled
Hamish McHamish of St Andrews:
Cool Cat About Town.

Robert Burns (1759-1796) is Scotland's most famous poet

Use the grid to carefully copy this image of Robert Burns.

Every year on the 25th of January many Scottish folk in Scotland and around the world celebrate his birthday with a Burns Supper.

Use funky colours to give this well-known image of Robbie Burns a modern twist.

The Scottish flag is known as The St Andrew's Cross, or The Saltire.

It depicts a white diagonal cross on a blue background. It is said to be one of the oldest flags in Europe. Many artists experiment with flags to create their own design.

Refashion the Scottish flag

The Scottish Colourists

'Peonies in a Chinese Vase'
by George Leslie Hunter (1877-1931)

The Scottish colourists were influenced by the French impressionist and post impressionist painters. They began using colour in a much more vibrant way. The four main painters of this group are John Duncan Fergusson, Francis Cadell, Samuel Peploe and George Leslie Hunter.

Add pattern and colour to create your own still life picture in the style of one of the Scottish colourists.

Create your own still life masterpiece

Select and arrange a group of objects to create your own still life. Carefully draw the objects, add colour and pattern to your drawing.

Create your own Scottish Art Gallery

Artist tip:-
Stick to the
same design
all the way
around the
frame.

Decorate these borders
with repeating patterns to
create attractive picture
frames.

What can you
draw inside the
frames?

Silly Sheep

1

2

3

4

5

6

Draw some silly sheep

More silly sheep to draw

Try copying these

Draw a flock of sheep

Artist tip:— To add perspective draw sheep which are large near the baseline and smaller sheep in the middle or top of the picture.

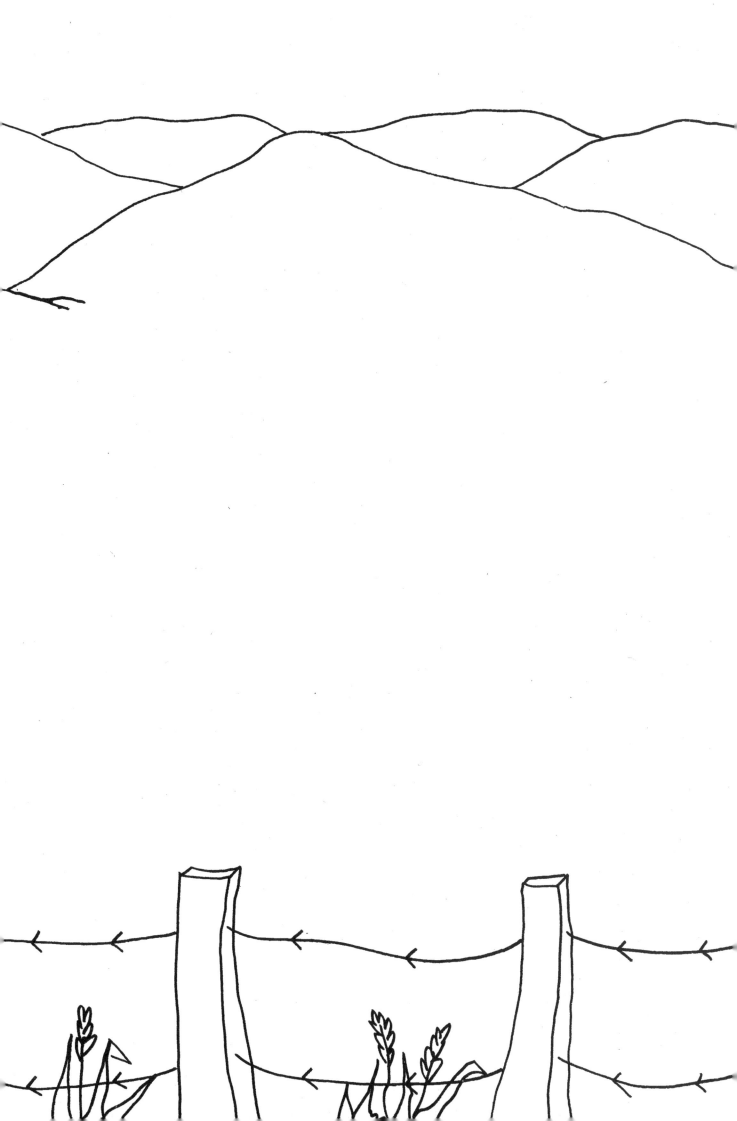

How to draw
a Westie

1

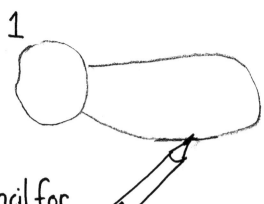

Use a pencil for
the basic outline.
Then use pen.

2

3

4

5

 Finally rub out
the pencil lines.

Try drawing your own Westie

1

2

3

4

5

The Scottish Wildcat

The Scottish wildcat is an endangered species. It is estimated there may be less than one hundred left in the wild, living in remote parts of Scotland. It can be difficult to tell them apart from the domestic cat but they can never be tamed, are bigger in size

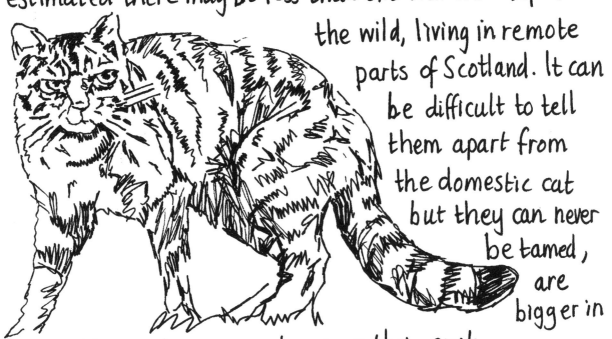

and have distinct markings on their coat.

It is perhaps the characteristic thick black stripes on their large, rounded tail which makes them more easy to recognise from the common tabby cat. The Scottish wildcat is a protected species. It is thought that one of the main reasons for their decline is due to them cross breeding with domestic cats.

Wildcats can be found in different places in Scotland including forests and moorland.

Wildcats have night vision that is seven times better than ours.

Wildcats have dark stripes to help them hide, this is camouflage.

Wildcats are excellent jumpers and are very fast runners.

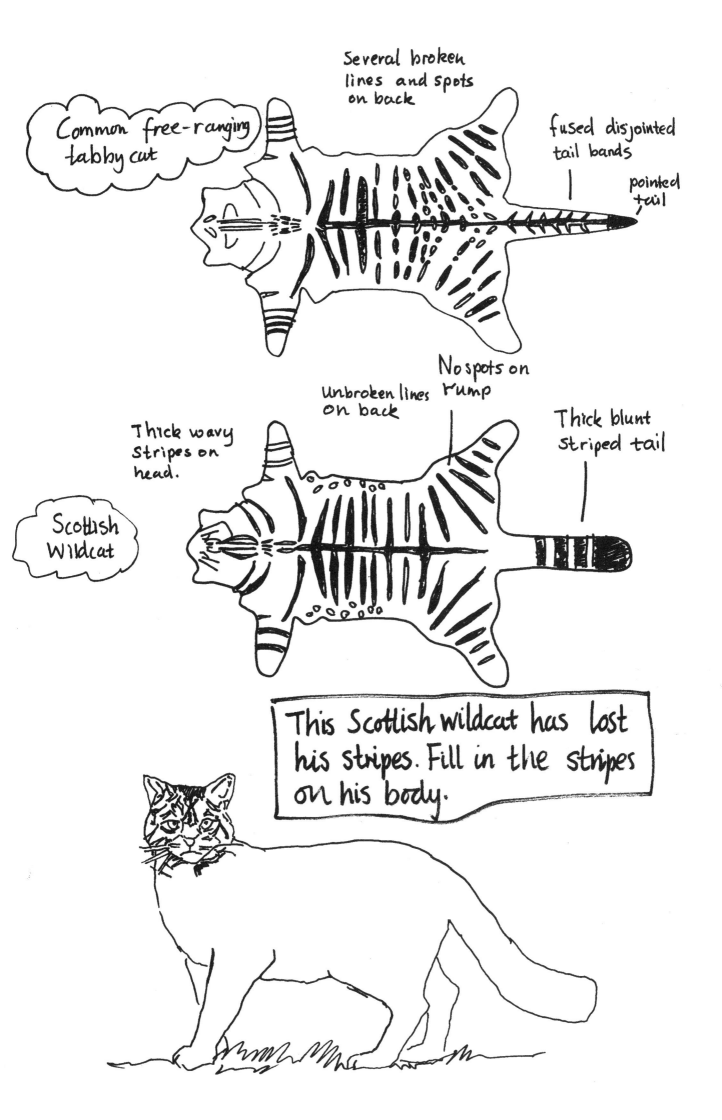

How to draw a Scottish Wildcat

1

Draw outline with pencil. then use a pen

2

3

4

5

6

7

8

Rub out pencil lines

Draw your own
Scottish Wildcat

This monochrome drawing was inspired by Sir Edwin Landseer's painting The Monarch of the Glen. Try colouring over the top to create a different mood.

Sir Edwin Landseer (1802-1873)

The English artist Edwin Landseer was a great favourite of Queen Victoria. He is famous for his paintings of animals. He spent a lot of time in Scotland which provided the subject matter for many of his most important paintings.

The Monarch of the Glen

Landseer's painting The Monarch of the Glen, an oil painting on canvas is perhaps one of Scotland's most well-known and iconic paintings.

Try creating your own version of The Monarch of the Glen

1. Draw into and colour the image of the stag.

2. Draw and colour some grasses along the baseline which would cover the stag's feet. These images should be detailed as they are at the front of the picture.

3. Draw hills behind the stag. Use blues and purples to create the ultimate chocolate box image of Scotland: a majestic stag set against the violet hills with a watery sky.

This abstract design is based on a golden eagle flying over the Scottish landscape. continue the design on the opposite page ⇒

Scotland is famous for weaving

Try Paper Weaving

1. Mark out lines as such on a sheet of thick paper or card.

2. Cut along the marked lines taking care not to cut all the way to the edge.

3. Cut out paper strips.

4. Use a simple over under pattern to create your own weave.

Draw evenly spaced lines.

The Outer Hebrides of Scotland have become famous for a beautiful woven cloth called Harris Tweed.

Try weaving with different materials such as newspaper, string or wool.

The Border towns of Galashiels, Hawick, Jedburgh and Selkirk are also well known for weaving.

The city of Aberdeen has become famous
for its oil. Evidence of this can be seen
around the coast which
competes with the
fishing industry and the unique
Scottish wildlife.

Finish this picture of a busy Aberdeen coastal scene.

Tenement Flats

Traditionally most of the working 'folk' living in the larger Scottish cities such as Glasgow, Edinburgh, Aberdeen and Dundee would live in a tenement flat or block.

These tenements often have beautiful tiling patterns decorating their hallways or closes.

This is a tiling design from the wall of a close in Tollcross, Glasgow.

A tessellation is a pattern made from geometric shapes, called tiles. There are no spaces inbetween the shapes.

Complete this tessellating pattern.

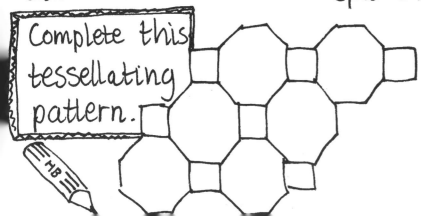

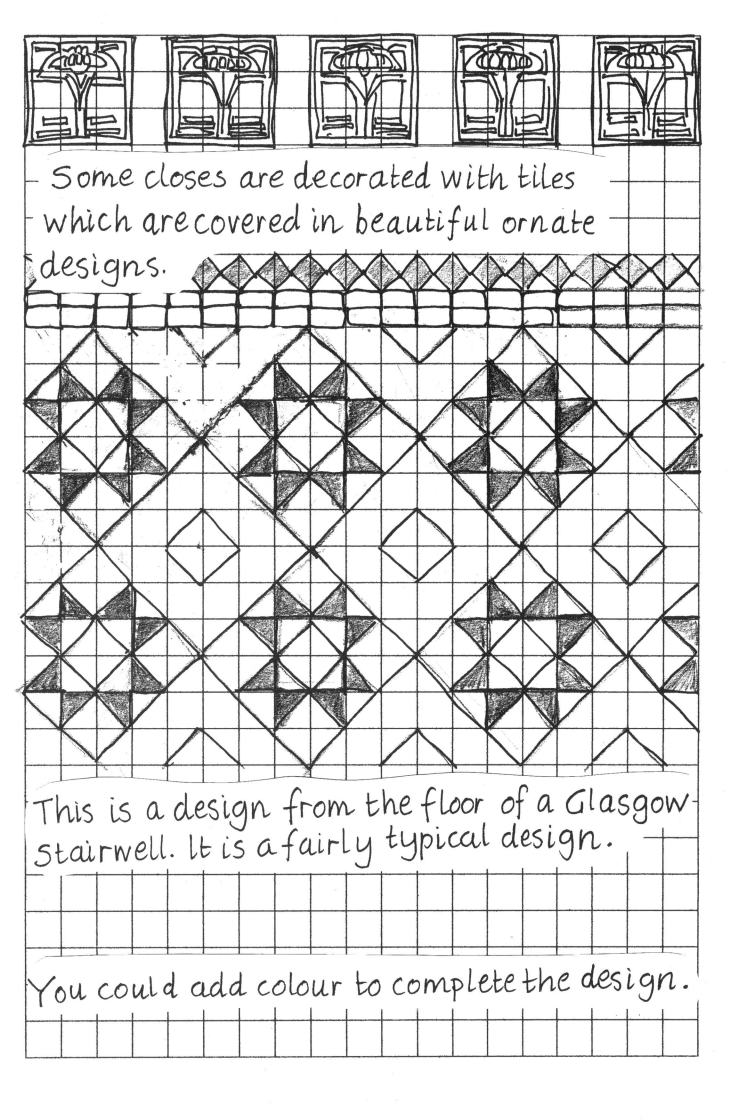

Some closes are decorated with tiles which are covered in beautiful ornate designs.

This is a design from the floor of a Glasgow stairwell. It is a fairly typical design.

You could add colour to complete the design.

Create more tiling designs.

Experiment by drawing designs on individual tiles.

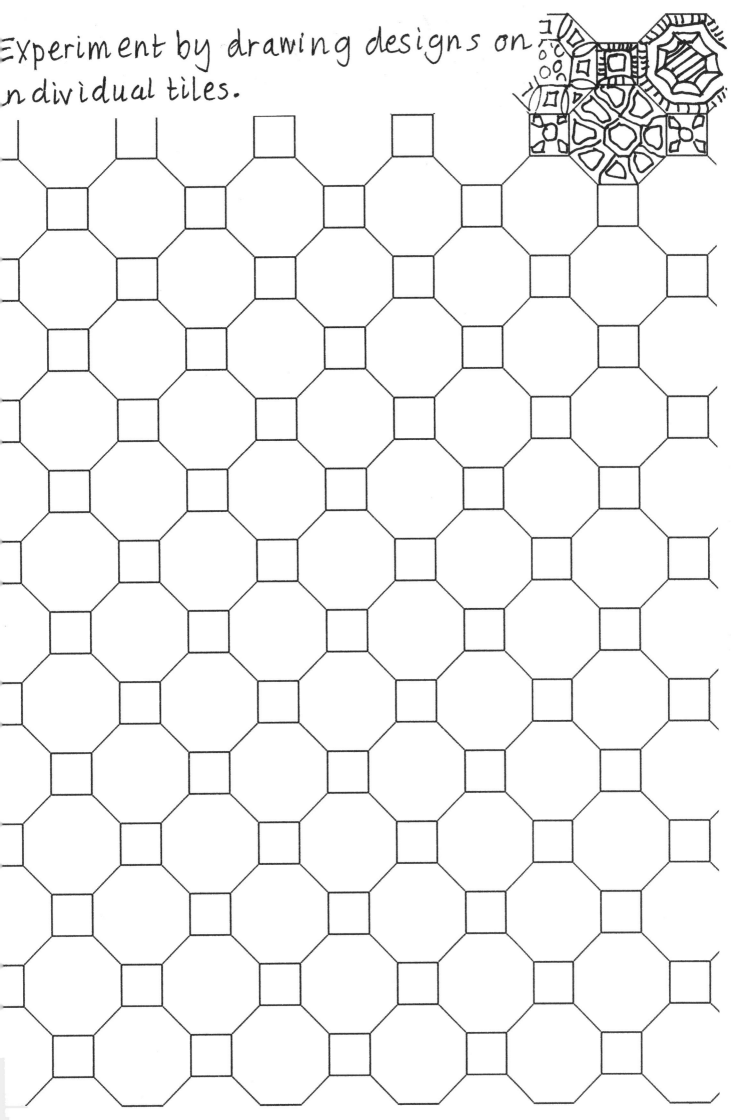

Create more tiling designs

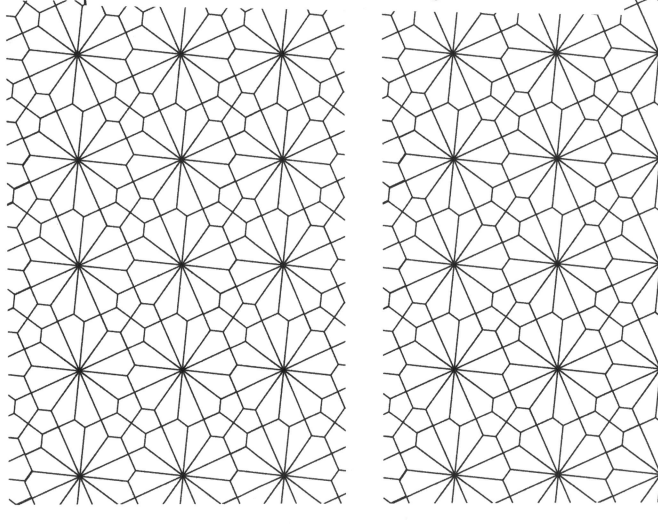

Midges are tiny wee beasties (insects) which are particularly common in the north west of Scotland. They usually gather in crowds and seem to enjoy biting humans!

Who are the midges chasing now?

ESTD
1797

Dundee

Dundee is famous for the three Js - jute, jam and journalism. The last jute mill closed in the 1970s but journalism and jam still play an important part in modern Dundee.

Design your own packaging, branding

and flavour for a new jam.

How to draw a Giant Panda

① ② ③ ④ ⑤ ⑥

Tian Tian and Yang Guang have been gifted to Edinburgh Zoo for 10 years.

Try drawing your own Giant Panda

Nessie - The famous monster living in Loch Ness

Nessie swimming

Nessie taking a walk

Climbing Ben Nevis

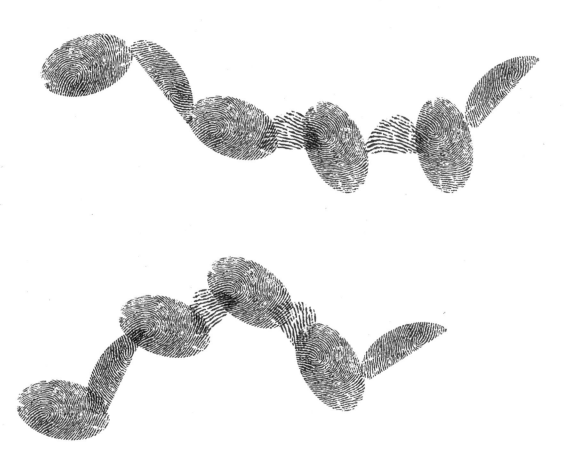

Some very Scottish fingerprints

Haggis Definition — a small creature with shorter legs on one side of its body so that it is able to run around the hills more easily.
To most people, the haggis is a delicious Scottish food, best served with neeps and tatties.
(turnips and potatoes)

A toast to the haggis

HB

More very Scottish fingerprints

a highland coo

Westie

puddock

Edinburgh Zoo's pandas

More very Scottish fingerprints

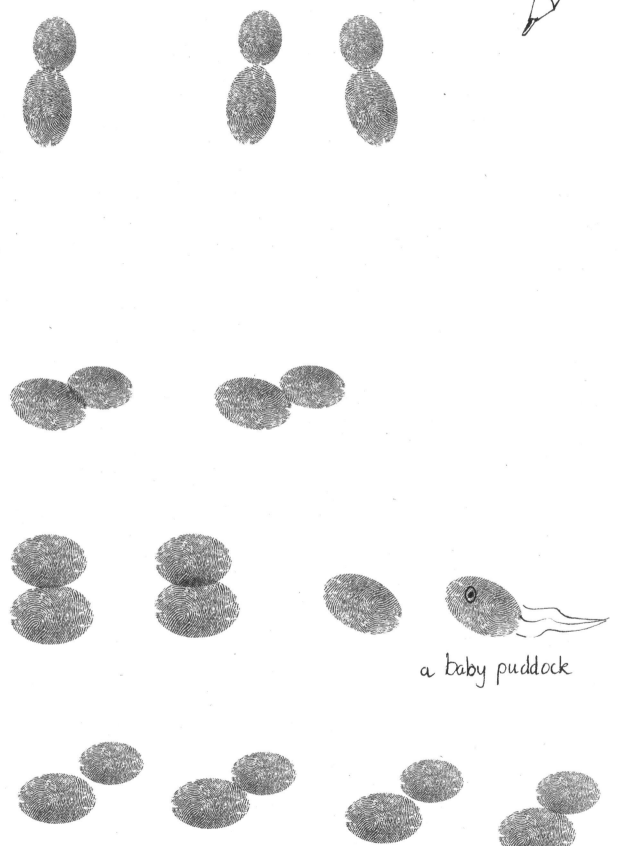

a baby puddock

A Shetland pony

Create more finger print designs.

The fly was drawn using
a black pen, a 2B pencil
and coloured with felt pen.

The salmon was drawn on top of newspaper using
a black pen and a 4B pencil.

This is a mixed media drawing. This means it was created using a variety of different materials. Finish the picture any way you like using any materials you like.

Seagulls can be found all over Scotland even inland.

Seagulls

Drawing on newspaper

You try drawing on newspaper

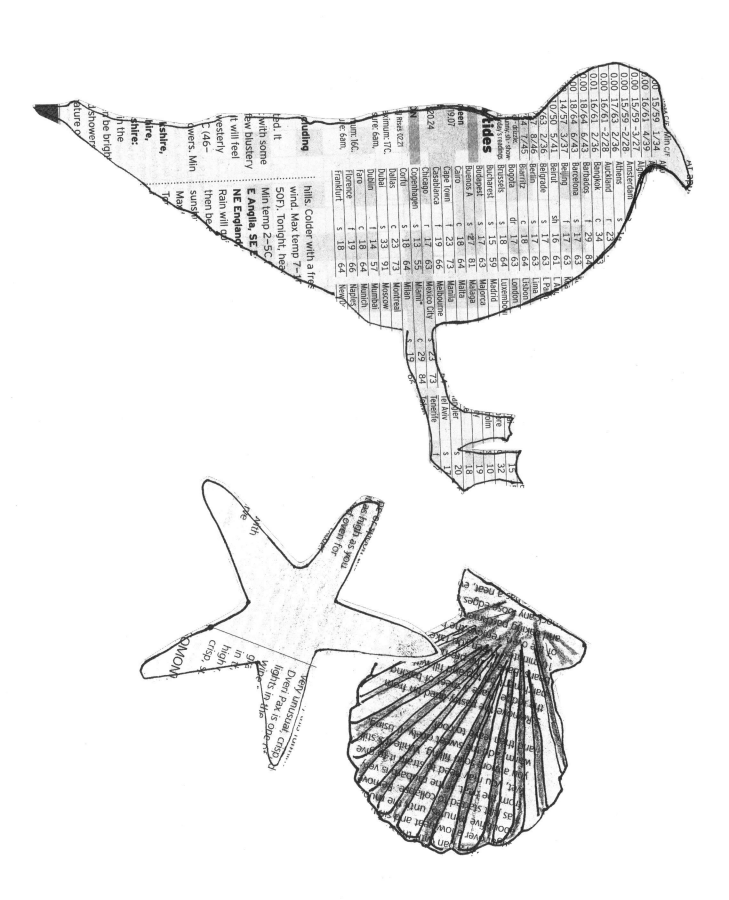

Brightly coloured fishing boats are often seen

...bing along the coast of Scotland.

decorate the fish

Who or what are the midges annoying?

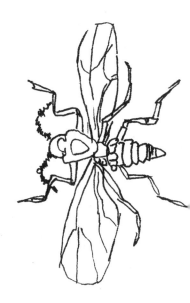

The thistle is the emblem of the Scottish nation. It may only be a humble weed but along with tartan it is perhaps the most identifiable symbol of all things Scottish.
Legend has it that a Norse army were about to ambush a party of sleeping Scottish warriors. The attackers, who were barefoot, stood on thistles. Their screams woke the sleeping Scots who were then able to defeat the invading army.
Hence the thistle was adopted as the symbol for Scotland.

O'flower of
Scotland

Complete this design

This simple design of a highland dancer was done using this technique.

Take your pen for a walk

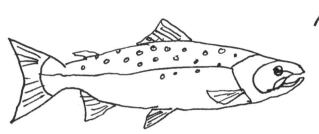

A salmon

A thistle

A Westie

Take your pen for a walk and create some
more Scottish images.

Lots more wee things to draw

The Scots Pine

Think of an unusual way to colour this sketch of a simple Scots pine tree.

Kelburn Castle, Largs in Ayrshire

In 2011 the author and designer Tristan Manco named the graffiti art project at Kelburn Castle as one of the world's top 10 examples of street art.

Add bright colour to finish this drawing.

raffiti art HB

Decorate these maps of Scotland

o create unique designs

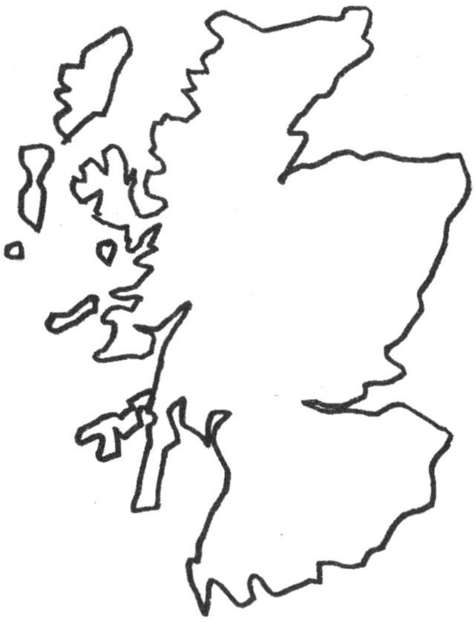
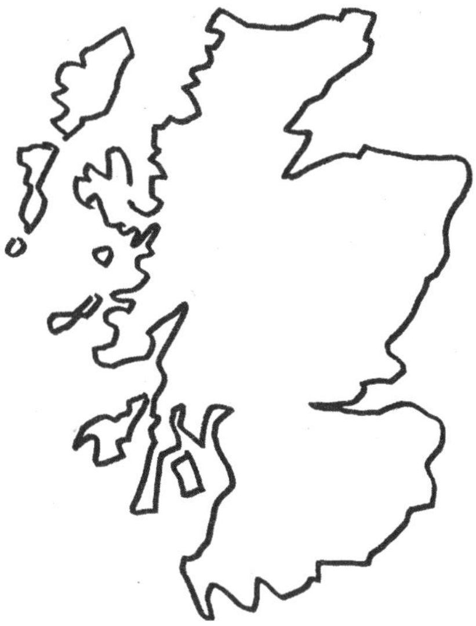
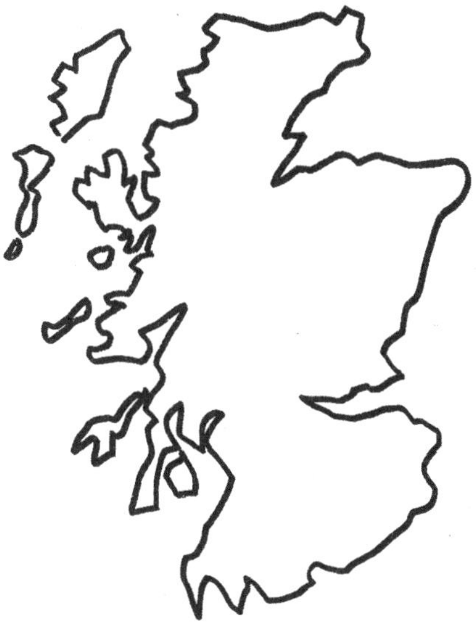
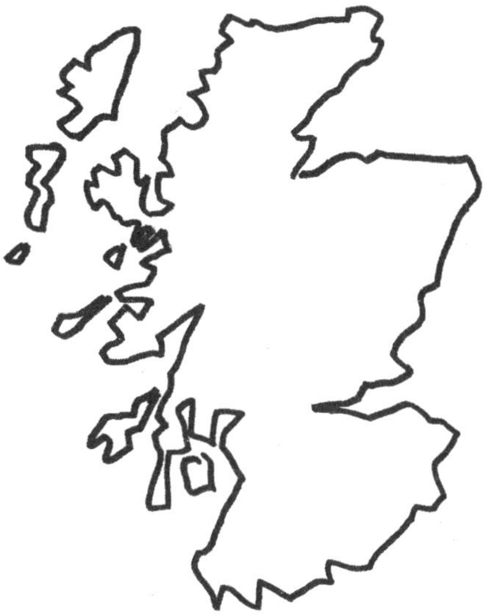
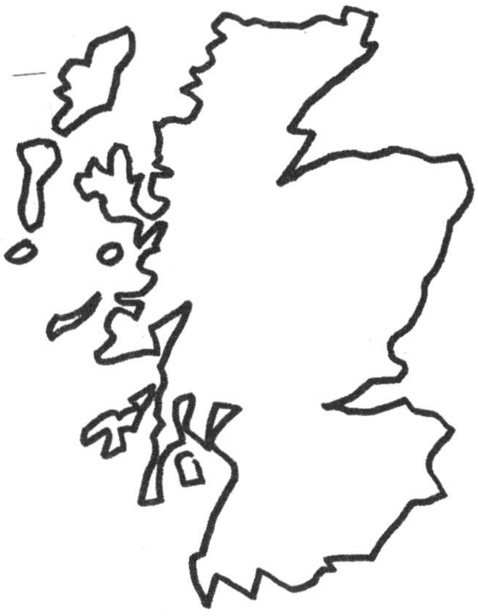
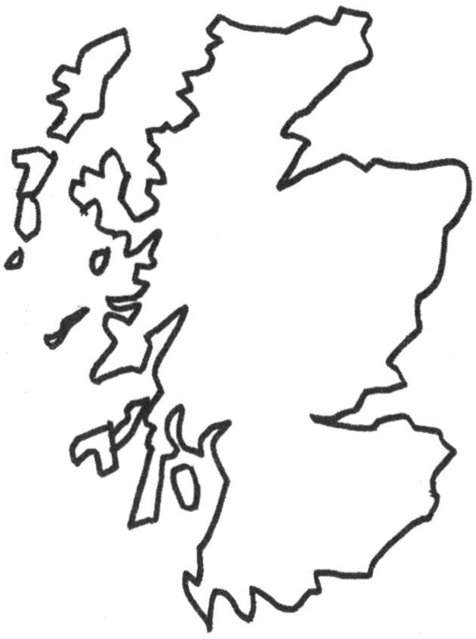
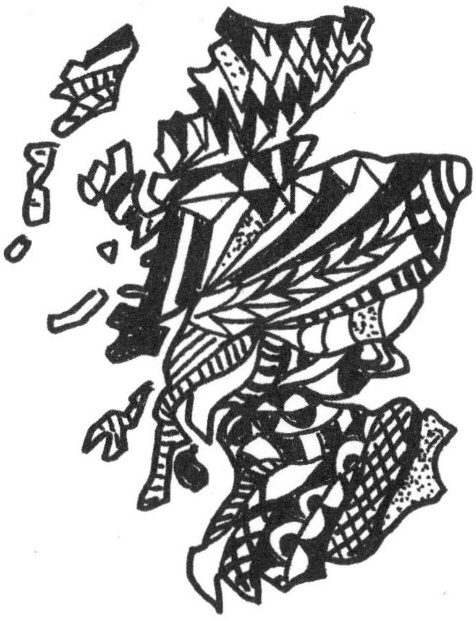
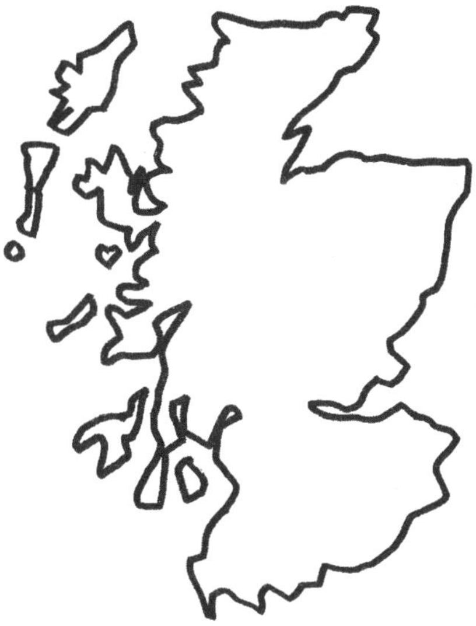
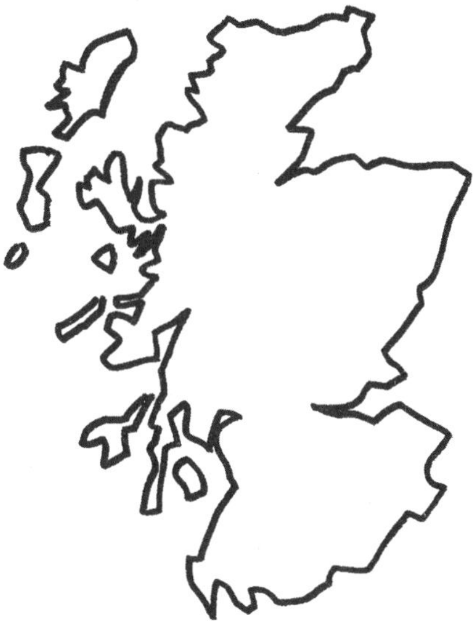

Edinburgh
Glasgow
Aberdeen
Stirling
Edinb
Perth

St. Andrews

Finish

Glasgow

rgh

Dundee

For Alice and Ellen who were the inspiration for this book.

Thank you John Peden, for having faith and encouraging me on this journey.

Thank you Brian Page for all the technical help!

Not forgetting Christine Page

Thank you

John Thomson

Norman Watson

Ian Campbell

Primary School pupils of Clackmannanshire

Anna Mackenzie

Black & White Publishing

Yvette Walker was born in Leeds and moved to Scotland with her family when she was 9. She studied Fine Art Drawing and Painting at Duncan of Jordanstone College of Art. After graduating she won an Art scholarship for her paintings, exhibited widely throughout Scotland and trained to be a primary teacher in Dundee.

For the past 10 years she has been involved in teaching Art in schools in Clackmannanshire, Scotland. She has had considerable experience teaching at all stages within the primary sector. The work in this book is a reflection of this.